T0149654

Power to Prevail Over the Battles Of Life

REV. I. D. SAMUEL

authorHOUSE

AuthorHouse™
1663 Liberty Drive
Bloomington, IN 47403
www.authorhouse.com
Phone: 1 (800) 839-8640

Published by AuthorHouse 08/09/2018

ISBN: 978-1-5462-5487-4 (sc)
ISBN: 978-1-5462-5486-7 (e)

Print information available on the last page.

KJV
Scripture taken from The Holy Bible, King James Version. Public Domain

Amplified Bible (AMP)
Copyright © 2015 by The Lockman Foundation, La Habra, CA 90631. All rights reserved.

CONTENTS

Introduction.. vii

Dedication xiii

Acknowledgements...xv

Chapter 1   What is Prolong Case File?................................. 1
Chapter 2   Further Examples of Prolong Cases................................. 13
Chapter 3   Testimonies of Victories Over Battles of Life................... 20
Chapter 4   Total Victory Over The Battles of Life........................... 26
Chapter 5   Principle For Dealing With the Battles of Life 31
Chapter 6   *Stronghold of Evil Prophecies* 44

About the Author... 59

INTRODUCTION

"Now there is at Jerusalem by the sheep market a pool, which is called in the Hebrew tongue Bethesda, having five porches.

In these lay a great multitude of impotent folk, of blind, halt, withered, waiting for the moving of the water.

For an angel went down at a certain season into the pool, and troubled the water: whosoever then first after the troubling of the water stepped in was made whole of whatsoever disease he had.

And a certain man was there, which had an infirmity thirty and eight years.

*When Jesus saw him lie, and knew that he had been **now a long time in that case**, he saith unto him, Wilt thou be made whole?*

The impotent man answered him, Sir, I have no man, when the water is troubled, to put me into the pool: but while I am coming, another steppeth down before me.

Jesus saith unto him, Rise, take up thy bed, and walk.

And immediately the man was made whole, and took up his bed, and walked: and on the same day was the sabbath.

*The Jews therefore said unto him that was cured, It is the Sabbath day: **it is not lawful for thee to carry thy bed.**"* (John 5:2-10)

A. Background

The Jews said to the man who had been in this protracted case for thirty-eight (38) years that because it is Sabbath day *"..it is not lawful for thee to carry thy bed"* (John 5:10). This implies that this man should not be set free today because there is a hold placed on his case.

Satan can use human beings to stand against or put a hold on a person's healing, deliverance, breakthrough, education, job and marriage. He usually presents evidences to support the case to stop his victim in order to hinder God's plans for their lives. This man's prolong case file of troubles of thirty-eight (38) years had been there even before Jesus was born

B. BETHESDA - "House Of Mercy"

Bethesda means the house of mercy. This man had been in the place of mercy for thirty-eight (38) years and yet never connected with God's mercy. Of the multitude of people by the pool none was ready to show him any kind of mercy. He wallowed in pain and denial for so many years till Jesus showed up with heavenly mercies.

Even though all that the bible tells us about him is that he is **"the impotent man"** but to what degree we did not know, we could only infer. One thing is clear however, he was suffering. What he was suffering from kept him from walking while some other fellows got their help from others, his own was a different case all together. His freedom was not forthcoming because satanic case had been opened filed against him. His case file was loaded with accusations that even he himself probably did not know anything about.

The enemy terminated his destiny and permanently sidelined or detained him among the weak, sickly, lame, paralyzed, hopeless, and helpless folks. There was a physical law in operation in the lives of those sick people there, but this man's case was different. He carried a high level of disfavor and his destiny portion was suspended until Jesus showed up.

Even when Jesus intervened he also almost missed his opportunity. When the Master saw him lying there he *"...knew that he had been **now a long time in that case ...**"* For this reason, his case for mercy and help from above had been settled by heaven. So when the Master asked him *"Wilt thou be made whole?"* It was just a question that did not demand any suitable answer. Whether he gave the right answer or not his matter had been settled. Mercy and favor located him and it was time to terminate thirty-eight years of affliction.

Hence, when the *"...impotent man answered him, **Sir, I have no man, when the water is troubled, to put me into the pool: but while I am coming, another steppeth down before me.**"* The Lord ignored this **impotent man's** focus on the **help of man** - because the help of man will fail him. Heaven was ready to heal him no matter what so *"**Jesus saith unto him, Rise, take up thy bed, and walk.**"*.

There was no need for argument, heaven had spoken, and so he rose took up his bed and began to walk: *And immediately the man was made whole, and took up his bed, and walked: and on the same day was the sabbath."*

The moment the power of heaven showed up in mercy to free this man from thirty-eight years of bondage, the law of man kicked in to challenge a man whom they ought to rejoice with. Instead of praising God and worshipping the Lord who set him free, the shocking news that followed is that:

*"The Jews therefore said unto him that was cured, It is the sabbath day: **it is not lawful for thee to carry thy bed.**"* (John 5:10)

They were technically correct but divinely in error and contrary to the mind of Christ. In Jeremiah 17:21-22 we read about the first law:

*"**Thus saith the** LORD**; Take heed to yourselves, and bear no burden on the sabbath day, nor bring it in by the gates of Jerusalem;**"*

Neither carry forth a burden out of your houses on the sabbath day, neither do ye any work, but hallow ye the sabbath day, as I commanded your fathers."

This law held every one of them there bound, and the Jews strictly enforced it. Remember other sick, helpless, paralyzed and weak folks were there but because of this law none of them made any effort to cry out for help or mercy. To receive from God you must approach the throne of grace, in order to obtain mercy (Hebrews 4:16)

Unknown to them He that had the divine order, and is the epitome of the true and real MERCY OF GOD had come to them but the physical law was holding all of them back. Even the one that mercy knocked at his door almost missed it. Yet in the presence of Jesus Sabbath did not count any more, hear Him in Mark 2:27-28:

*"And he said unto them, **The sabbath was made for man, and not man for the sabbath:** Therefore the **Son of man is Lord also of the sabbath.**"*

The Son of Man (Jesus) is Lord also over the Sabbath, therefore Sabbath has no preeminence over Him. Furthermore, in Isaiah 1:13-15 God had earlier spoken about His objections to the religious zealots about His opinion on the matter:

*"**Bring no more vain oblations; incense is an abomination unto me; the new moons and sabbaths, the calling of assemblies, I cannot away with; it is iniquity, even the solemn meeting.***

Your new moons and your appointed feasts my soul hateth: they are a trouble unto me; I am weary to bear them.

And when ye spread forth your hands, I will hide mine eyes from you: yea, when ye make many prayers, I will not hear: your hands are full of blood." (Isaiah 1:13-15)

"I will also cause all her mirth to cease, her feast days, her new moons, and her sabbaths, and all her solemn feasts." (Hosea.2:11)

In spite of the revelatory truth above, Satan had been taking advantage of the ignorance of people to oppress them. The enemy of God Satan has been working against the church with the same laws, rituals, and forms of religion that violate the words of God, and he exalts pride and hypocrisy to hinder God's acts of mercy and love for His children,

Later on after the encounter, Jesus revealed to the man thereafter the secret behind his case through the second law in John 5:14:

"Afterward Jesus findeth him in the temple, and said unto him, Behold, thou art made whole: sin no more, lest a worse thing come unto thee."

Jesus told him the reason behind the prolong attack over his life - it was as a result of sin. God told Cain that sin is waiting for him at his door and that sin has a desire to hold him. Sin torments physically but spiritually it is a force of destruction that holds his victim bound. Sin bound this man for thirty-eight (38) years. Human laws and legalism fastened the nail of the coffin of his affliction.

Human laws and legalism are hindrances to divine purpose. Never mind, heaven had spoken concerning the impotent man, and there was nothing the law keepers could do about it. Beloved concerning you too God's word is settled in heaven no matter the case file opened against you, mercy shall prevail for you in Jesus name.

DEDICATION

This book is dedicated to Jesus my savior and the Holy Spirit, my comforter whom the father (GOD) has sent in His name, and the one who teaches me all things, and brings all things to my remembrance, whatsoever He have said unto me (John 14:26)

ACKNOWLEDGEMENTS

With a total heart of gratitude, I graciously appreciate and acknowledge my spiritual parents who laid a great spiritual foundation for my life - Rev. (Dr.) O. Ezekiel of Christian Pentecostal Mission International (CPM), under whose crusade ministry I was saved and Rev. Dr (Mrs.) M. Ezekiel the National/International Codinator of CPM, who by God's anointing upon her life through the Faith Clinic program made me what I am today in spiritual warfare.

I will also not forget the following spiritual giants, my mentors Pastor Benny Hinn, Pastor Wale Oladiyun, Bishop Henry Saliu, Pastor Taiwo Ayeni, Dr. Elizabeth Vaughn, Dr. Diana Brown, I also specially acknowledge my wife Pastor Joy Ifeanyi Samuel and my godly treasures, Chijioke Samuel, Mercy Nnenna Ogechi Samuel, Ebubechi Nwa Samuel, Chibuike Samuel, Favour Chiamaka Samuel, Precious Chimzurum Samuel. Pastor Juliana Ucheoma, Pastor Daniel Ucheoma, Pastor Bethrand Onochie etc who have all blessed my life and all the members of Living Victorious Life INT'L Ministries.

CHAPTER ONE

What is Prolong Case File?

"And a certain man was there, which had an infirmity thirty and eight years.

*When Jesus saw him lie, and knew that he had been **now a long time in that case**, he saith unto him, Wilt thou be made whole?*

The impotent man answered him, Sir, I have no man, when the water is troubled, to put me into the pool: but while I am coming, another steppeth down before me.

Jesus saith unto him, Rise, take up thy bed, and walk.

And immediately the man was made whole, and took up his bed, and walked: and on the same day was the sabbath." (John 5:5-9)

Background

From the scriptures above we read that when Jesus saw the man lying down on his bed, he knew he was ***now a long time in that case.*** The man was obviously confronted with a debilitating case beyond his control. He needed a greater power or force to procure his deliverance.

For thirty-eight years he was an abandoned case with no man to help him inside the water when the angels come to trouble it. He had waited for that day, in this prolong case of hopeless and helpless infirmity, when help would come from above until Jesus miraculously showed up out of mercy to heal him. So now what is prolong case file?

1) it's a stubborn situation or occurrence in somebody's life, which calls for serious or urgent attention. It's an evil attachment that the enemies never want to let go.

2) A specific evil occurrence that requires a serious spiritual investigation, and higher authority to deal with it.

3) It's a satanic spiritual law suit or action filed against a person demanding legal or illegal claims over that life and everything he or she lays hands on.

4) An evil hand that consistently and persistently meddles in a person's life, thereby interfering in every path leading towards fulfilling God's desires in that life.

5) An evil mark, stamp or imprint spiritually placed in someone's life unknown to him or her.

6) A satanic stronghold that exalts itself against God's plans or assignment upon people's lives here on earth thereby causing inexplicable hindrances or delays.

7) Satanic blockage at the edge of break-through in a person's life

8) It is failure at the edge of success, and non-accomplishment in a person's life.

9) It is a lifestyle of having great dreams, visions, or desires of great things but never seeing the realty

10) Going through unending wars and battles that are diabolically inspired from the pits of hell.

11) It is satanically organized battles and manipulations from infancy against people's lives.

12) A satanic summons or vow pronounced to make someone fail in almost every area of his or her life.

13) It's an arrow of downfall shot from hidden ancients altars against people in all they do in life.

14) Satanic mandates and judgments holding evil evidences of avengers against some-one's life, marriage, career or jobs, etc.

15) It is satanic bitter writings from generational past still holding evil retaliations against the present lifestyle of their victims. (Job 13:26)

16) It is demonic agents holding satanic documents or evidences of parental vows, promises, oaths, or covenants made in the past against their victims.

17) It is ancient satanic stumbling block and wicked reinforcement that has been pushing people down at the moments of their advancements.

18) It is evil foundational entanglement responsible for failures and delays in people's families.

19) It is hidden strange altars networking with any environment people find them-selves to keep resisting them from entering into God's plans for their lives.

20) It is an unending deployment of evil spies conducting evil investigations, and evil monitoring that help them to keep records and evidences of peoples' past.

Bible Examples

1. **In Psalm 109:6** we read *"Set thou a wicked man over him: and let Satan stand at his right hand."* This is a biblical reference and evidence showing the opening of case files against Satan's victims.

2. **Daniel**

In the book of Daniel Chapter 10 verses 11-14 we read the account of how the Prince of Persia withstood the angel bringing Daniel's message to him: *"But the prince of the kingdom of Persia withstood me one and twenty days: but, lo, Michael, one of the chief princes, came to help me; and I remained there with the kings of Persia."* (v13)

This Principality kept Daniels's blessings from reaching him for twenty-one days. Imagine if Daniel had stopped praying!

3. **JOB 1:6-19** (AMP)

The case of Job is revealed to us in Job 1:6-19, how Satan (adversary, accuser) came one day before the Lord with the sons of God and:

"The LORD said to Satan, "From where have you come?" Then Satan answered the LORD, "From roaming around on the earth and from walking around on it."

The LORD said to Satan, *"Have you considered and reflected on My servant Job?*

For there is none like him on the earth, a blameless and upright man, one who fears God [with reverence] and abstains from and turns away from evil [because he honors God]."

Then Satan answered the LORD, "Does Job fear God for nothing?

Have You not put a hedge [of protection] around him and his house and all that he has, on every side? You have blessed the work of his hands [and conferred prosperity and happiness upon him], and his possessions have increased in the land."

From the account above, Satan had been walking around Job looking for loopholes to open up a case file against him in order to attack him for a long time before now. However, God's hedge of protection over Job, his family and all that belonged to him kept Satan in abeyance for that long until God gave him the permission to test Job.

"But put forth Your hand now and touch (destroy) all that he has, and he will surely curse You to Your face."

Then the LORD said to Satan, "Behold, all that Job has is in your power, only do not put your hand on the man himself." So Satan departed from the presence of the LORD.

God's permission gave Satan the power to open a case file of afflictions against Job and all that belonged to him. We saw in the rest of the account how satanic afflictions took away his children, some of his servants, oxen, sheep, donkeys and camels. Satan used the Sabeans, Chaldeans, lightning and winds of destruction to decimate all that Job possessed. Furthermore, in Job 2:1-10 we see how Job himself was personally afflicted with boils:

"So Satan departed from the presence of the Lord and struck Job with loathsome boils and agonizingly painful sores from the sole of his foot to the crown of his head."

At this time, even if doctors all over the world gathered together to medically treat job on his ailments there was nothing much they could have done to help him because a spiritual case file had been opened against him and Satan and his agents were at work in his life.

In spite of his pain he never accused God of wrong doing. But his wife could not handle it. The frustration of her pain and loss made her to wrongly misinterpret what was happening to her family.

"Then his wife said to him, "Do you still cling to your integrity [and your faith and trust in God, without blaming Him]? Curse God and die!"

But he said to her, **"You speak as one of the [spiritually] foolish women speaks [ignorant and oblivious to God's will]. Shall we indeed accept [only] good from God and not [also] accept adversity and disaster?"**

In [spite of] all this Job did not sin with [words from] his lips."

Like Job, all that the wife ought to have done at that time was to

"Be sober, be vigilant; because your adversary the devil, as a roaring lion, walketh about, seeking whom he may devour." (1 Peter 5:8)

She failed God by speaking unadvisedly with her mouth.

4. **The Conspiracy Against Daniel**

In Daniel 6:7-24 all the presidents of the kingdom, the governors, and the princes, the counselors, and the captains, all conspired together to establish a royal statute, and to make a firm decree, that whosoever shall pray to any God or man for thirty days, with the exception of the king shall be cast into the den of lions.

"Now, O king, establish the decree, and sign the writing, that it be not changed, according to the law of the Medes and Persians, which altereth not." (v8)

King Darius signed the writing and the decree, not knowing it was a trap set to put Daniel into the lion's den. Daniel who was aware of their evil intentions never protested but trusted the Lord whom he diligently served without wavering to deliver him. When he knew that the decree was signed, it did not deter him, but: "**.....he went into his house; and his windows being open in his chamber toward Jerusalem, he kneeled upon his knees three times a day, and prayed, and gave thanks before his God, as he did aforetime.**" (v10).

He opened the windows of his house and prayed not minding what Satan and his agents would do.

Meanwhile, predictably enough, they knew that Daniel would fall for their trap because no matter how dangerous the conditions might be Daniel would still pray to his God. So *"Then these men assembled, and found Daniel praying and making supplication before his God."* (v11).

Their immediate response was to go to the king and insisted that Daniel be put in the lion's den *"...according to the law of the Medes and Persians, which altereth not."* (v12)

The King now realizing his error we are told in verse 14 was angry at himself *"and set his heart on Daniel to deliver him: and he laboured till the going down of the sun to deliver him."*

In spite of the king's efforts to deliver Daniel, the case file that Satan opened through his palace agents was at work, hence after intense pressure he gave in commanding that Daniel be put in the den of lions. Then the king said to Daniel, *"Thy God whom thou servest continually, he will deliver thee."* Thereafter, a stone was placed there and sealed it with his signet and that of his Lords so that Daniel's case could never be averted. (v16-17).

Then he went to his palace to begin all night prayer and fasting for Daniel. He was the first to get to the den to find out whether Daniel made it, and to the glory of God he did and his enemies who conspired against him with all their households replaced him in the den of lions (v18-24). Beloved no matter how bad your case and that of your family may be, be rest assured in your spirit that power is available to terminate it through intense prayer and fasting in Jesus name.

5. **Joshua and the Resistance of Satan**

We read in Zechariah 3:1-7 how Satan stood to challenge the authority of Joshua the high priest while ministering before the Lord *"...and Satan standing at his right hand to resist him."* The right hand is a place of power and authority, no wonder we are told in Psalm 110:1 to sit at God's right hand until he makes our enemies our footstool. So Satan knew where to stand to cripple the priest of God, whom he falsely accused in order to afflict him. But in verse 2 of the scriptures we read:

"And the LORD said unto Satan, The Lord rebuke thee, O Satan; even the LORD that hath chosen Jerusalem rebuke thee: is not this a brand plucked out of the fire?"

Why was Satan able to have the audacity to attack a priest of the Lord? As we read in verse 3 the man of God opened himself to attack, he "........*was clothed with filthy garments, and stood before the angel.*"

But thank God for His mercies who intervened for Joshua who had found mercies in the hand of the Lord who: "*....answered and spake unto those that stood before him, saying, Take away the filthy garments from him. And unto him he said, Behold, I have caused thine iniquity to pass from thee, and I will clothe thee with change of raiment.*"

The Lord commanded "*Let them set a fair mitre upon his head. So they set a fair mitre upon his head, and clothed him with garments. And the angel of the LORD stood by.*" (v5).

Thereafter, the Lord said unto Joshua, saying, "*Thus saith the LORD of hosts; If thou wilt walk in my ways, and if thou wilt keep my charge, then thou shalt also judge my house, and shalt also keep my courts, and I will give thee places to walk among these that stand by.*"

These requirements are salient factors that are important to God so much that God did all He could to set his record straight, and that if Joshua would meet the standard He would place him in His purpose for his life. No matter the distraction of Satan, God is able to restore one to the path of life and righteousness.

6. Satanic Attacks on God's Vessel

a) **Peter**: The plan of the devil is to mess up God's vessel in the assignment of the kingdom of God. We see in Luke 22:31-32

"And the Lord said, Simon, Simon, behold, Satan hath desired to have you, that he may sift you as wheat:

But I have prayed for thee, that thy faith fail not: and when thou art converted, strengthen thy brethren."

In the verses above, we can see how Jesus prepared for the deliverance of Peter, but he almost missed it because of over confidence and arrogance. Instead of taking the advice of the Lord, he resisted divine counsel and said *"......Lord, I am ready to go with thee, both into prison, and to death. And he said, I tell thee, Peter, the cock shall not crow this day, before that thou shalt thrice deny that thou knowest me."* (v33-34).

Peter failed because he discountenanced the word of the Lord. So when the due season came and he was challenged about his relationship with the Lord, he denied knowing Him and just as the Master said the cock did not crow that day before Peter denied Him thrice. Peter remembered the words of the Lord and in verse 62 we read: *"And Peter went out, and wept bitterly."*

b) **Judas** - While in the case of Peter there was divine remedy, Judas was not that blessed. Even though the Master warned that someone would betray Him, Judas like Peter took it lightly and Satan easily perfected his case file for afflicting him.

Even when all the other disciples *"..were exceeding sorrowful, and began every one of them to say unto him, Lord, is it I?"* Judas' response tepid at the best and all he said was *"..Master, is it I? He said unto him, Thou hast said."* (Matt 26:20-25)

It wasn't therefore a surprise in Luke 22:3-4 where we read that:

"Then entered Satan into Judas surnamed Iscariot, being of the number of the twelve. And he went his way, and communed with the chief priests and captains, how he might betray him unto them."

He was largely unprepared for the package of assaults and afflictions Satan put in his case file, and for this reason his story did not end well. Even though when the cloud settled, and saw that Jesus was condemned to death he felt bad that he betrayed the Lord. He repented of his sin and returned the thirty pieces of silver to the Chief Priests and elders but what he heard from them did not inspire him to wait for the fruit of repentance to kick in. So he went out and hanged himself. Before his death however, we heard Judas

"Saying, I have sinned in that I have betrayed the innocent blood. And they said, What is that to us? see thou to that. And he cast down the pieces of silver in the temple, and departed, and went and hanged himself." (Matt 27:4-5)

He committed suicide.

Fiery Prayers

1) Holy spirit of God grant me access to commune with you, lead and strengthen me on how to pray now in Jesus name.

2) Holy spirit of God, reveal to me now what I need to know that I don't know about prolong evil affliction against my life in Jesus mighty name.

3) Holy spirit of God, restore unto me every good information for my next level in God's plans for my life, ministry, business, jobs, career, breakthroughs, and progress that I have lost in Jesus name.

4) Holy Spirit of God through your power and grace mortify my life and body to live a holy life unto you in Jesus.

5) Holy Spirit of God, grant unto me fresh grace for a prayerful lifestyle and uphold me in walking on your divine plans for my life.

6) O Lord let every of my little effort in life provoke a great harvest for my next level and let nothing be left undone on your assignment for my life.

7) Every evil horse and chariot of war assigned to hinder my progress and stop God's assignment for my life catch fire and burn to ashes in Jesus name.

8) O Lord takeover the battlefield of my life and may your hands be visible than my effort in Jesus mighty name.

9) O Lord God use all your creative power to help me against prolong battles over my life in Jesus mighty name.

10) I command a nullification of every oath and vow of my parents in the past generations unknown to me that may still be existing, and influencing me in any area of my life, to make me hewers of wood and drawers of water to others in life.

11) I challenge those parental oath and vows with their evil covenant as I stand on the blood of Jesus and the new covenant in Christ Jesus, and command them to lose their claims over my life in Jesus mighty name.

12) O Lord expose and destroy every evil and crafty plot of the enemy set to take place in any particular hour, day, week, month and year against any area of my life in the mighty name of Jesus.

13) Every satanic barrier visible or invisible and traps set out against me to delay God's plans for my next level in life, be destroyed out of my way in Jesus name

14) Any organized satanic legislative meeting going on to delay God's plans for my next level in life, be scattered in seven different ways in Jesus mighty name.

15) Every satanic network of age-long evil cases causing delays against any area of my life, be scattered in Jesus mighty name

16) Every evil congregation using any material to consult against my life to delay God's plans for my next level, be scattered and destroy yourselves together in Jesus mighty name

17) Every evil power and demonic agent gathering evidences against my life to delay God's plans for my move to the next level, be paralyzed and scattered in Jesus mighty name

18) Every witchcraft activity operating secretly to hinder God's plan for my life, marriage, business, advancement, promotion education, ministry, and church I command you to fail woefully in Jesus mighty name.

19) Every evil bird, reptile, insect, and animal programmed to cause delays and troubles in my marriage, business, jobs, education, ministry, promotions, and church, I curse you to die in Jesus mighty name

20) All evil associations of wicked and satanic elders speaking afflictions into my life, marriage, business, education, progress, success, ministry, and church I command you to receive the judgment of death in Jesus mighty name.

CHAPTER TWO

Further Examples of Prolong Cases

"And he was teaching in one of the synagogues on the sabbath.

And, behold, there was a woman which had a spirit of infirmity eighteen years, and was bowed together, and could in no wise lift up herself.

And when Jesus saw her, he called her to him, and said unto her, Woman, thou art loosed from thine infirmity.

And he laid his hands on her: and immediately she was made straight, and glorified God." (Luke 13:10-13)

A glorious occurrence like this is an opportunity to rejoice and praise God for the great things He had done for this woman bound for eighteen (18) years. But what happened thereafter through the mouth of the ruler of the synagogue revealed how so much unhappy Satan was about the deliverance of that woman. All he could point out was that Jesus healed the woman in violation of the Sabbath saying in anger:

"...There are six days in which men ought to work: in them therefore come and be healed, and not on the sabbath day.

The Lord then answered him, and said, Thou hypocrite, doth not each one of you on the sabbath loose his ox or his ass from the stall, and lead him away to watering?

And ought not this woman, being a daughter of Abraham, whom Satan hath bound, lo, these eighteen years, be loosed from this bond on the sabbath day?(Luke 13:14-16)

Please take note of what Jesus said. All He was saying to the people was that 'wasn't this proper that the daughter of Abraham whom Satan had held bound for this eighteen (18) years should be set free?' Satan through the ruler of the synagogue still had the audacity to lay charges against this woman in spite of Jesus' prayer of deliverance to set her free. Beloved, whatsoever charges or case that Satan may raise against you, hold on to the finished work of grace and maintain your deliverance or healing.

What happened to that woman similarly applies to us today if you have given your life to Christ. You belong to Jesus Christ, therefore every charge or case file with any evidence Satan has against you, using them as strongholds to torment you through sickness, and poverty, is already nullified in Jesus name. If there is also the spirit of disfavor, causing disagreement between you and some people or if there are any unknown wicked activities against your life they have also been nullified through the work on the cross.

Because you have been set free through the finished work of Christ Jesus on the cross, it is now over to you to exercise authority over the devil and his agents in any area where they are waging wars against you whether it's your marriage, your health, education, jobs, business, and progress etc. But because of the lack of knowledge amongst some believers, Satan has been using their ignorance to hold them captive. However, the promise of Christ's atonement is revealed to us in Romans 5:8-11.

"But God commendeth his love toward us, in that, while we were yet sinners, Christ died for us.

Much more then, being now justified by his blood, we shall be saved from wrath through him.

For if, when we were enemies, we were reconciled to God by the death of his Son, much more, being reconciled, we shall be saved by his life.

And not only so, but we also joy in God through our Lord Jesus Christ, by whom we have now received the atonement.

Life is a journey, a race and a mystery full of battles which the only winners are those on God's side. The good news is that you are here on earth for God's assignments, and it's not in any way in God's mind to see you stuck in all the affairs of your life. However, there are unseen evil case file that the enemy had opened against you and which had been at work against you for a very long time. The enemy has refused to let go off your life and progress placing on your paths snares, pitfalls, wicked seduction, deceptions, entrapments, or entanglements. These all are wired against your marriages, fruits of the womb, businesses, families, progress, breakthroughs, prosperity, success etc.

For this reason, he has succeeded in presenting his certificate of ownership and certificate of stock marks to so many people all over the world, binding the lives and destines of many of them. He has kept many bound using the assigned instruments of strongholds of poverty, hardship, disfavor and a life full of lack of accomplishments in all areas of life. He has thereby made many who have for long desired achievements in areas of their lives to give up after they failed to come to pass.

Spiritually, a lot of people are unknowingly going about with stock marks over their lives. Marks of limitation, impossibilities, failure at the edge of success and stagnation yet they do not know about them. It's sad. But if you're a born-again child of God, I have good news for you because your case will end in praise, and you are about to move into the next level of your life as God planned for you. There is power of God available for you to escape every satanic allegation placed against you and to win all his prolong evil case filed against you. Power is also available to defeat him and his agents who spiritually filed the cases against you.

Friend many of the problems people are going through in life are as a result of satanic summons against them. But life is in classes, in sizes and levels and no matter your class, size and level right now there is always another higher class, size and higher levels ahead of you according to the word of God in Proverbs 4:18: *"But the path of the just is as the shining light, that shineth more and more unto the perfect day."*

No matter how bad the summons against you may be, as long as you remain in Christ your path shall remain shining till Christ comes. We are truly reassured in 1 Corinthians 2:9

*"But as it is written, **Eye** hath **not seen**, nor ear heard, neither have entered into the heart of man, the things which God hath prepared for them that love him."*

There are things unseen and unknown to you that God has packaged for you in this life and they are ahead of you. There is always room for progress in every child of God's life and also at every level of life there are battles to fight before moving into your next level. But we see many times how adversaries will come to make sure you never get to your next level on time or totally stop you. This situation is the same for many people who have made moves to cross to their next level. They have unexpectedly been confronted with challenges in health, in business, in marriage, in ministry, etc. in the process. While others face similar challenges and overcome, theirs will linger for years and decades. So many times many of these unfortunate folks go to their graves with it because an evil hand had opened a case file against them vowing never to let go.

"Thus saith the LORD of hosts; The children of Israel and the children of Judah were oppressed together: and all that took them captives held them fast; they refused to let them go.

Their Redeemer is strong; the LORD of their cause, that he may give rest to the land, and disquiet the inhabitants of Babylon." (Jeremiah 50:33-34)

May God also plead your cause and grant you freedom in Jesus name. Amen

Fiery Prayers

1) Every unfriendly friend secretly sponsoring problems into my life, marriage, business, jobs, success, progress, education, ministry, and church to hinder God's plans for my life, be exposed and destroy yourself in Jesus mighty name.

2) By the power in the blood of Jesus, I break from my family the evil cycle of affliction working against any area of my life in Jesus mighty name.

3) Every monitoring and wicked evil affliction trailing me in any area of my life be destroyed without remedy in Jesus name.

4) All stubborn parental wicked evil force sponsoring satanic embargo on my marriage, business, jobs, education, future and career, by the authority in the blood of Jesus be silenced forever in Jesus mighty name.

5) O Lord grant me quick justice and vindicate me from every evil allegation my enemies are raising against me in Jesus mighty name.

6) I bind and destroy every dark power assigned to supervise any evil case filed against me in the name of Jesus.

7) Every evil decree from the pit of hell issued against me while I was still in my mother's womb be nullified in the name of Jesus.

8) Every shame, reproach or disgrace operating against my life from infancy till date as a result of evil accusation raised against me by the enemies in my lineage, be canceled and removed by the blood of Jesus.

9) By the authority in the blood of Jesus, I nullify the operations of every bar of iron and the fetters of brass limiting my progress, success, promotions, and marriage in Jesus mighty name.

10) By the authority in the blood of Jesus, I cancel and break off every spell, curse, jinx, evil covenant and enchantment working against me as a result of evil case filed against me.

11) I command God's destructions on every evil searcher and hunter of my stars in Jesus mighty name.

12) By the authority in the name of Jesus Christ, I claim permanent victory over all the haters and persecutors of my life and greatness in Jesus mighty name.

13) Every gathering set up to raise evil accusation against my life, be scattered without remedy in Jesus name.

14) Every satanic agent submitting documents of evil allegations against me, by the authority of the blood of Jesus be destroyed without remedy in Jesus name.

15) I decree the anger of God to arise and pursue all evil pursuers raising satanic accusations against any area of my life in Jesus mighty name.

16) O arise for my help and turn all the struggles, ridicules and obstacles coming against me from evil case filed against me unto miracles in Jesus name

17) I command every path to my breakthroughs to be opened by the authority in the name of Jesus.

18) Every evil altar of demotion erected by the enemies of my soul be shattered to pieces without remedy in Jesus name.

19) O Lord by the authority that is in the blood of Jesus, I declare all forms of worldliness, carnality and compromises that opened evil case files against my life to be destroyed in Jesus mighty name.

20) By the authority in the blood of Jesus I destroy every activity of spiritual luke-warmeness, shallowness, and prayerlessness that is empowering any satanic accusation against my life in Jesus name

CHAPTER THREE

Testimonies of Victories
Over Battles of Life

"....but Hannah had no children." (1 Samuel 1:2)

"Hannah prayed, and said, My heart rejoiceth in the Lord, mine horn is exalted in the Lord: my mouth is enlarged over mine enemies; because I rejoice in thy salvation.

There is none holy as the Lord: for there is none beside thee: neither is there any rock like our God.

Talk no more so exceeding proudly; let not arrogancy come out of your mouth: for the Lord is a God of knowledge, and by him actions are weighed.

The bows of the mighty men are broken, and they that stumbled are girded with strength.

They that were full have hired out themselves for bread; and they that were hungry ceased: so that the barren hath born seven; and she that hath many children is waxed feeble." (1 Samuel 2:1-5)

1) Hannah

If people have concluded that there is no hope for you, let them wait until you return from reading this book, then their language about you shall change. Just like Hannah you'd sing a new song, and the Lord shall cause your mouth to be enlarged over your enemies; because you'd rejoice in God's salvation. Hannah had waited in fasting, refusing to eat until she opened her heart unto the Lord with whom she drove a hard bargain of giving the child back to God if God answered her.

"And she was in bitterness of soul, and prayed unto the LORD, and wept sore.

And she vowed a vow, and said, O LORD of hosts, if thou wilt indeed look on the affliction of thine handmaid, and remember me, and not forget thine handmaid, but wilt give unto thine handmaid a man child, then I will give him unto the LORD all the days of his life, and there shall no razor come upon his head. (1 Samuel 1:10-11)

God did and the rest became the history of her testimony.

2) The Shunamite Woman

".....And Gehazi answered, verily she hath no child, and her husband is old.

And the woman conceived, and bare a son at that season that Elisha had said unto her, according to the time of life." (2 Kings 4:13, 17)

This was the story of a woman who had personally given up hope of ever having a child, but God used her giving to reconnect her with her miracle. Having taken good care of Elisha, the man of God desired to reward her but the woman was not excited about it as we read in 2 Kings 4:16:

"And he said, About this season, according to the time of life, thou shalt embrace a son. And she said, Nay, my lord, thou man of God, do not lie unto thine handmaid."

In spite of her reaction the word of God concerning her in heaven was settled, so as we read in v17:

"And the woman conceived, and bare a son at that season that Elisha had said...."

Elisha's prophetic prayer broke the barriers of satanic limitation over her life. This is to let you know no matter how prolonged your case may be, when God is ready for you, your victory is certain and you shall testify in Jesus name.

3) **Jabez**

The power of prayer cannot be over-emphasized as we see prayer power again at work in the life of Jabez in 1 Chronicles 4:9-10

*"And Jabez was more honourable than his brethren: and **his mother called his name Jabez, saying, Because I bare him with sorrow**. And Jabez called on the God of Israel, saying, oh that thou wouldest bless me indeed, and enlarge my coast, and that thine hand might be with me, and that thou wouldest keep me from evil, that it may not grieve me! **And God granted him that which he requested**."*

God honored him and He *"... **granted him that which he requested**."*

4) **The Healing of The People**

In Luke 6:17-21, the profound encounter there reveals the desperation of a great multitude of people who came out to hear him and were healed of their diseases. Even those that were oppressed by demons were also set free and Jesus in His message to them made a profound statement:

*"Blessed are ye that hunger now: for ye shall be filled. **Blessed are ye that weep now: for ye shall laugh**."* (Luke 6:21)

The fastest way to your turn around is through your hunger for righteousness, and your brokenness in weeping shall translate to victory and laughter. Therefore,

"When the LORD turned again the captivity of Zion, we were like them that dream. Then was our mouth filled with laughter, and our tongue with singing: then said they among the heathen, The LORD hath done great things for them.

The LORD hath done great things for us; whereof we are glad. (Psalm 126:1-3)

Fiery Prayers

1) All organized demonic evil case files networked against my spiritual, matrimonial, financial lives, progress, success, education, and jobs be nullified by the authority that is in the blood Jesus.

2) Every organized evil case filed against me, working days and nights, to hinder God's plans upon my life, by the authority in the blood of Jesus be nullified in Jesus might name.

3) All organized satanic sanctions against my advancement in life, ministry, business, home, and job be nullified by the authority that is in the blood of Jesus.

4) Every satanic network of evil case causing ungodly delays on the path to my next level rising of God's plans for my life be nullified and scattered without remedy in Jesus mighty name.

5) I nullify and destroy every evil agent using any physical material in consulting against my well being in life in Jesus name.

6) I paralyze and destroy the powers of demonic agents set against my welfare and progress in life in Jesus name.

7) By the authority that is in the blood of Jesus I nullify and destroy satanic rituals and sacrifices offered against my progress and success in life in Jesus name.

8) In the name of Jesus I nullify and scatter every witchcraft accusation, and evil network secretly operating against me within my neighborhood, home, church and business.

9) By the authority in the blood of Jesus I paralyze and destroy all stubborn demonic prophets working on evil case filed against me.

10) In the name of Jesus I bulldoze out of my way every mysterious satanic accusation hindering my way to God's plans for my life.

11) I remove by force and fire every stumbling block of evil accusation against my next level rising in Jesus name.

12) Every satanic assault system from evil case filed against me that is resisting my well being in life be neutralized by the authority in the blood of Jesus Christ.

13) In the name of Jesus I forcefully remove every mysterious satanic blanket covering my glory.

14) All altars of darkness inspired by evil case filed against my success, church, job, business and are still speaking be silenced in Jesus mighty name.

15) Every power of evil that has vowed to tie down my future, business, finances, church, home, and marriage in shame and disgrace be destroyed in Jesus mighty name.

16) I command the satanic arrangement of evil limitation hindering God's plans for my life to fail woefully and be destroyed in Jesus mighty name.

17) Every satanic hideout within me and around my home, church, business be exposed and destroyed in Jesus name.

18) All satanic fighters commissioned to destroy me as a result of evil case filed against me be paralyzed and destroyed in Jesus mighty name.

19) Any gifts I have given which evil agents are using as evidence against me be nullified and rendered impotent by the authority in the blood of Jesus Christ.

20) In the name of Jesus I destroy any image representing me, my business, church, and job.

CHAPTER FOUR

Total Victory Over The Battles of Life

This prayer booklet is written to help you acquire God's knowledge of how to prevail over the battles of life, and eliminate all prolong evil cases of satanic afflictions filed against you. You would be able to confront or fight against all areas of your life that the enemies have placed his evil siege and embargos. Embargos that have hindered God's plans for your life, and those stubborn barriers or cobwebs of the enemies set up to frustrate God's given assignments over your life. Let us together review the steps to victory in the battle against the forces of darkness.

1. **Knowing Your Right**

The first step to your total freedom or victory over prolong evil case filed against you is **knowing your right in the finished work of Calvary.** You must know your identity in Christ, your knowledge in Christ, and not just your knowledge about your place in Christ but your experience in Him. This is because your knowledge about your position in Christ is the story acquired, while your knowledge of your position in Christ is your personal experience of what Christ has done and what He can do again for you. Proverbs 11:9 confirms that it's "..*through* ***knowledge*** *shall the just be delivered.*" And Isaiah 5:13 equally confirms that "..*my people are gone into captivity, because they have no* ***knowledge****:....*"

2. Knowing The Right Direction to Run

In the journey of life, no matter how fast you run in the wrong direction, you will never get to your rightful destination. Hence, the full knowledge of God's purpose and plans on your life, how to follow Him and His principles are all you require for your total victory over prolong battles of life.

God is a God of principles, and not following His principles for answered prayers is like running the race of life in the wrong direction. There are principles you must apply if you desire quick results for your prayers. God's power is available for you to win all prolong evil cases filed against you, and that power is to know His ways and principles of doing things. And your following His ways and principles are the keys to your deliverance from prolong battles you're engaged in against satanic forces.

3. Receiving Revelation Through Praise

In Psalm 50:23 we read:

*"Whoso **Offered praise glorified me**; and to him that ordered his conversation aright **will I shew the salvation of God**."*

Prayer is a conversation between you and your father in heaven, and it's not one way but two way communication between two personalities. Until you see prayer that way, your prayer life will just be informative (one way) rather than communicative (two way) exchange. Your prayer life won't be successful, if there is no desire for feedback.

From the scripture above the word of God tells us that whosoever channels his or her life aright as he prays, God will show that person His hands of salvation. This means any time you aligned your prayer life aright with God's purpose, He will reveal to you His saving, healing and deliverance powers to you. He will respond to your request, because you have met His expectation of the right person praying. This also means people can pray wrongly. I want to encourage you to follow His leading or direction and you shall have testimonies.

Following Him aright would end forever your days of praying amiss and you'd be a partaker of His revealed promises that should make your journey to fulfilled purpose easier.

"...And truly He shall shew (you) the path of life: in (His) presence is fulness of joy; at (His) right hand there are pleasures for evermore." (Psalm 16:11)

Fiery Prayers

1) I destroy by force and fire every satanic reinforcement using unknown doors to gain access into my life in Jesus mighty name.

2) Every power reinforcing the judgment of evil case ordered against any area of my life is terminated in Jesus mighty name.

3) In the name of Jesus I forcefully dismantle every satanic structure and pillar sustaining the operations of the judgment of evil case filed against me to be rendered impotent and useless in the name of our Lord Jesus Christ.

4) I scatter in the name of Jesus all satanic reinforcement deployed daily to resist God's plan for my life.

5) In the name of Jesus, I forestall the regrouping of satanic agents continuously holding false allegations against my life in order to set me up for perpetual affliction.

6) Every satanic voice crying downfall against my home, business, job, education, church and ministry be silenced in Jesus mighty name.

7) By the authority in the blood of Jesus Christ I arrest and destroy in Jesus mighty name every satanic armed robber delegated from the gates of hell to steal, kill and destroy.

8) By the authority in the mighty name of Jesus Christ, I declare the spirit of confusion and stubborn quarrelling into the midst of wicked counselors set against my life.

9) Every transfer of evil case file from my ancestors challenging my present life, family, business and ministry be terminated and destroyed in Jesus mighty name.

10) By the authority in the blood of Jesus Christ, all foundational inheritance of evil cases from my parents challenging my progress, success, church, ministry, and job release your grips over my life in Jesus mighty name.

11) Every wicked power supervising evil cases filed against any area of my life by the authority in the blood of Jesus Christ, be nullified and destroy in Jesus mighty name

12) By the authority in the blood of Jesus Christ, I paralyze all aggressive agents working with evil agents set against any area of God's plans for my life in Jesus mighty name.

13) Every evil stone of backwardness, hardship and stagnation placed against any area of my life by the agents of evil be forcefully removed and scattered in Jesus mighty name.

14) Every hand of afflictions from evil case files preventing God's plans for my life be paralyzed and destroyed in Jesus mighty name.

15) Every demonic barrier network through the air, sun, and moon to frustrate God's plans for my life be nullified and scattered in Jesus mighty name.

16) By the authority in the blood of Jesus Christ, every evil handwriting and satanic ordinances from evil case files against God's plans upon any area of my life be paralyzed and scattered in Jesus mighty name.

17) Any unknown satanic initiations done against my pictures, clothes, monies or anything that represent me both physically and spiritually be nullified and destroyed in Jesus mighty name.

18) Every generational or ancestral barrier erected anywhere holding back all my destiny needs for my advancement be nullified and destroyed in Jesus mighty name.

19) Every terrible cloud from evil case file assigned to follow me around from my infancy be nullified and scattered without remedy in Jesus mighty name.

20) Any invisible siege surrounding my advancement in life, ministry, church, business, and job be nullified and scattered in Jesus mighty name.

CHAPTER FIVE

Principle For Dealing With the Battles of Life

"For whatsoever is born of God overcometh the world: and this is the victory that overcometh the world, even our faith." (1 John 5:4)

A. Background

The Lord that we serve is a God that operates based on principles, and if we His subjects can diligently follow His ways it shall be well and good for us. Having a knowledge of His ways is very crucial, and using them effectively is even much more. That is the reason we are to review a few principles that would help us to overcome the challenges of the battles of life confronting us.

1) *BE GENUINELY BORN-AGAIN.*

Being genuinely born again grants you divine access to God. The bible tells us in 2 Corinthians 5:17 that: *"...if any man be in Christ, he is a new creature: old things are passed away; behold, all things are become new."* The newness of your life and walk with Him is what opens you up to victorious living as we read in 1 John 5:4:

"For whatsoever is born of God overcometh the world: and this is the victory that overcometh the world, even our faith." (1 John 5:4)

Not only that but as we also read in John 1:12 we are given the power to be called the sons of God.

"But as many as received him, to them gave he power to become the sons of God, even to them that believe on his name."

2) BE QUICK TO FORGIVE

We have all heard the saying "To err is human but to forgive is divine." This is true and confirmed in the words of our Lord in Mark 11:25-26.

"And when ye stand praying, forgive, if ye have ought against any: that your Father also which is in heaven may forgive you your trespasses.

But if ye do not forgive, neither will your Father which is in heaven forgive your trespasses."

We are also encouraged in Colossians 3:12 -13 to *"Put on therefore, as the elect of God, holy and beloved, bowels of mercies, kindness, humbleness of mind, meekness, longsuffering;*

Forbearing one another, and forgiving one another, if any man have a quarrel against any: even as Christ forgave you, so also do ye."

In a nutshell we can glean the following on forgiveness:

 a) Forgiveness relieves us of a burden we are carrying
 b) It frees one from a "prison of torment"
 c) Forgiveness closes a "door" that is allowing Satan and his agents access to one's life.
 d) It allows one to "step out of the way" and let God have a "direct line" to the offender

It is important for us to know that forgiveness should be more than just the blessings we are hoping to receive or benefits attached from "letting go" but we should forgive in obedience to God's word and because we also have been forgiven (Colossians 3:13).

Maturity in Christ comes with the exercise of the spiritual gifts within the word of God for us and "*speaking the truth in love*" (Ephesians 4:11–16). Sanctification comes through the Word of God we believe and put into practice (John 17:17).

3) *SHOW GRATITUDE*

The saying that if you're thoughtful you'd be grateful seems relevant here. Not only is it a necessary ingredient of quick answer to prayer and fellowship, God commanded it. For example in Colossians 3:15 we read:

"And let the peace of God rule in your hearts, to the which also ye are called in one body; and be ye thankful."

Giving thanks to God in appreciation to Him is part of a believer's worship. This same is expected in sustaining or making both old and new relationships work. Showing gratitude or appreciation is so crucial it is expected daily in our relationship with God, and it is connected with receiving answers to our prayers as we see in Ps 50:14-15.

*"**Offer unto God Thanksgiving***; *and pay thy vows unto the most High;*

*And call upon me in the day of trouble: I will deliver thee, and thou shalt **glorify me**."*

4) *HAVE FAITH IN GOD'S WORD*

Without faith in God's words our prayers will be a waste of time and energy. I want you to know that it's God's will to answer your prayers as His child. But God can only answer your prayer by your total obedience to His words and instructions. In fact, Faith is so important in answer to your prayer because without it, it is impossible to please Him. You must believe in Him you're praying to and that He's able to reward you as you diligently seek Him as we read in Hebrews 11:6:.

"But without faith it is impossible to please him: for he that cometh to God must believe that he is, and that he is a rewarder of them that diligently seek him."

Faith is an unseen force that makes its ability to get result in prayer available to us as we wait on God's word. Faith is able to help us do anything God desires us to do and it comes by having or establishing a strong relationship with God first.

What makes a relationship strong and sweet is the amount of time you're willing to invest or spend together in it. Spending time with each other makes the relationship between two people stronger. In the same way the closer you are to God and His words the more you have access to His will, and the revelation of His word.

Furthermore as the relationship with God grows the more you begin to know him and the more you keep sharing His thought. From this perspective, you start thinking in line with the way He thinks. Then by extension as you keep thinking like God you start behaving in the image and likeness of Him. Faith comes by staying in contact with God's word as we read in Romans 10:17:

"So then faith cometh by hearing, and hearing by the word of God."

Faith is having total confidence on God's words and what you say to yourself from what God says to you. If God says that you are healed then you turn and say to yourself God is not lying to me because I know Him, and I believe it, so that settles it - you're on the right track. Faith comes based on your knowledge of Him, not on what you know about God but what you really know Him for by experience and not assumption.

5) **POWER OF VOWS AND TITHE**

The one place where we see the power of vow positively work gloriously is in the prayer of Hannah to God in 1 Samuel 1:10-11;

"And she was in bitterness of soul, and prayed unto the LORD, and wept sore.

And she vowed a vow, and said, O LORD of hosts, if thou wilt indeed look on the affliction of thine handmaid, and remember me, and not forget thine handmaid, but wilt give unto thine handmaid a man child, then I will give him unto the LORD all the days of his life, and there shall no razor come upon his head."

God speedily answered her prayer and she fulfilled her vows as Job 22:27 tells us *"Thou shalt make thy prayer unto him, and he shall hear thee, and thou shalt pay thy vows."* In addition, verse 28 tells: *"Thou shalt also decree a thing, and it shall be established unto thee: and the light shall shine upon thy ways."*

It's important to mention, however, that it is very dangerous to vow and not fulfill it as it carries grave consequences. Keep your vows

"When thou shalt vow a vow unto the Lord thy God, thou shalt not slack to pay it: for the Lord thy God will surely require it of thee; and it would be sin in thee.

That which is gone out of thy lips thou shalt keep and perform; even a freewill offering, according as thou hast vowed unto the Lord thy God, which thou hast promised with thy mouth." (Deuteronomy 23:21, 23)

6) *RIGHTEOUS LIVING IS ESSENTIAL*

Who is the righteous one? The righteous one is the person who has been washed and cleansed by the blood of Jesus. This is the person who has received Him as Lord and savior. The righteous ones are the ones whom He has given the power to be called the sons of God, that is those who believe in His name (John 1:12). The promise of God to the righteous is blessing:

"For thou, LORD, wilt bless the righteous; with favour wilt thou compass him as with a shield." (Ps 5:12).

It is righteousness that gives the believer a right standing in the place of prayer. No wonder Psalm 66:18 states:

"If I regard iniquity in my heart, the Lord will not hear me:"

The book of Isaiah 59:2 also confirms the same:

"But your iniquities have separated between you and your God, and your sins have hid his face from you, that he will not hear."

Take note that the scriptures above confirm that righteousness is essential in answer to your prayers.

7) *ALIGNING YOUR WORDS WITH GOD'S WORD*

The word of God is powerful and it was with God from the beginning, and it was the power that inspired the creation of all that God called to being. In Genesis we are told that the spirit of God moved upon the face of the waters and nothing happened until God spoke (Gen 1:2-3). The word of God has creative ability, and He created man to possess the same grace. The gospel of John tells us in John 1:1 that

"In the beginning was the Word, and the Word was with God, and the Word was God."

The word of God is settled in heaven (Ps 119:89). The word as confirmed by the Lord in John 6:63 is spirit and life.

"It is the spirit that quickeneth; the flesh profiteth nothing: the words that I speak unto you, they are spirit, and they are life."

Proverbs 4:22 also confirms that the words of God are life unto those that find them, and health to all their flesh. God's word never fails; it accomplishes what it is sent to do.

"So shall My word be that goes forth out of My mouth: it shall not return to Me void [without producing any effect, useless], but it shall accomplish that which I please and purpose, and it shall prosper in the thing for which I sent it." (Isaiah 55:11 AMP)

Just as God's words don't fail, our words bear fruits when we speak them (Prov. 12:14; 13:2-3). We are warned in Psalm 34:12-13 that for us to see better days and long life, we must keep our tongue from speaking guile. Align your words with God's word for speedy answer to prayers. Many whose words do not align with God's words have been ensnared by their words *"Thou art snared with the words of thy mouth, thou art taken with the words of thy mouth."* (Prov 6:2)

8) *MEDITATING ON GOD'S WORD*

The two persuasive scriptures on meditation that reveals its benefit in helping one to become and grow are found in Joshua 1:8 and Psalm 1:1-3.

"This book of the law shall not depart out of thy mouth; but thou shalt meditate therein day and night, that thou mayest observe to do according to all that is written therein: for then thou shalt make thy way prosperous, and then thou shalt have good success." (Joshua 1:8)

"Blessed is the man that walketh not in the counsel of the ungodly, nor standeth in the way of sinners, nor sitteth in the seat of the scornful. But his delight is in the law of the LORD; and in his law doth he meditate day and night. And he shall be like a tree planted by the rivers of water, that bringeth forth his fruit in his season; his leaf also shall not wither; and whatsoever he doeth shall prosper." (Psalm 1:1-3)

They are both unarguably self explanatory and clear in what they express or present. You can never become anything worthwhile or prosper if you don't meditate. Meditation grows a person. Therefore meditate, be empowered and grow!

9) *BE DETERMINED TO FOLLOW GOD'S WAYS NOW AND AFTER YOUR PRAYER IS ANSWERED*

In Psalm 119:1-3 we are told that:

"Blessed are the undefiled in the way, who walk in the law of the LORD.

Blessed are they that keep his testimonies, and that seek him with the whole heart.

They also do no iniquity: they walk in his ways."

From the scriptures above, it is important to know that he that is undefiled in the way of the Lord, and walks based on God's word is blessed. When you choose to walk in the way of the Lord, you have refused to walk in the way of the ungodly (Ps 1:1) and there is great benefit in this. You must be resolute and settled in your mind to stand only where God stands and never shift ground for the devil in your fight. Be a dogged spiritual fighter, so that you can prevail over the battles of life. Prayer power is the secret.

Be a strong minded person who will never want to lose any battle to the devils and their agents. Like Daniel you must persevere in your fight till you win and come out victoriously every day of your life. Strive to develop formidable prayer power.

*"But **Daniel purposed in his heart that he would not defile himself** with the portion of the king's meat, nor with the wine which he drank:,,,"* (Dan 1:9)

10) *DEALING WITH THE BATTLES OF LIFE THROUGH PRAYER AND FASTING*

There is no better scriptures that define prayer and fasting than Psalm 40:1:

"I waited patiently for the Lord; and he inclined unto me, and heard my cry."

Fasting requires waiting, and not just waiting anyhow but waiting patiently. When you wait patiently you are intentional or deliberate declaring *"If I perish I perish."* (Esther 4:16).

The choice of waiting must be backed with determination and desperation. Make it a do or die business. No wonder Job 14:14 asked a rhetorical but profound question:

"If a man die, shall he live again? all the days of my appointed time will I wait, till my change come.".

Wait till you see your change come! There is nothing difficult for God to do if only you can wait on Him in prayer and fasting. Our God specializes in impossibilities, and He has handled cases harder than yours before, so choose to wait!

In fact there are biblical testimonies of those who came to God in fasting and in prayers with issues that look impossible to them but they left with new songs. The same God who did it for them is also able to do yours too.

The principles of prayer and fasting are great tools believers have to prevail over the battles of life. Applying both constructively is known as waiting on the Lord. It's a power instrument in handling stubborn evil cases, even Jesus confirmed their potency in Mark 9:29

"And he said unto them, This kind can come forth by nothing, but by prayer and fasting."

*"**Wait on the LORD**: be of good courage, and he shall strengthen thine heart: **wait**, I say, **on the LORD**."* (Psalm 27:14)

B. Reflections on Prayer and Fasting

Prayer and fasting in faith are without doubt the most powerful force on earth. If you are in good standing with God no matter how low you have fallen down into the pit of financial difficulties, marital problems, health challenges, and any other difficulties of life in any area of your life, the Lord will show up to help you.

With these two most powerful tools in your life as a child of God, glorious thing can happen again in your life. Prayer and fasting are unlimited forces without boundaries by time or space. They are powers that switch off anything that looks impossible and switch on power of possibilities.

In Mark 11:22-24 the Lord introduces us to the binding force that elicits answer to prayer, which is faith, and faith is now. Faith is now; while hope is of the future. Faith is a good receiver, while hope is a good waiter.

*"And Jesus answering saith unto them, **Have faith in God.***

For verily I say unto you, That whosoever shall say unto this mountain, Be thou removed, and be thou cast into the sea; and shall not doubt in his heart, but shall believe that those things which he saith shall come to pass; he shall have whatsoever he saith.

Therefore I say unto you, What things soever ye desire, when ye pray, believe that ye receive them, and ye shall have them.

And when ye stand praying, forgive, if ye ought against any: that your Father also which is in heaven may forgive you your trespasses."

C. Benefits of Prayer and Fasting

The benefits of prayer and fasting from a sincere heart to God as gleaned from Isaiah 58:7-12 are itemized below. When you fast you'd experience the following:

a) Every darkness around you will disappear and your light will shine.
b) Your health will spring forth speedily
c) The righteousness of God will go ahead of you
d) God's glory will be your rear guard
e) The Lord will guard you continually
f) The Lord will satisfy you in the time of drought
g) The Lord will make your bones fat, a healthy life
h) You will be like a watered garden at all times
i) All your waste places will be rebuilt
j) You will raise up the foundations of many generations
k) You will be called, the restorer of the paths to follow, living behind a legacy for others to follow.

Fiery Prayers

1) Every hidden evil spoiler using the power of evil case filed against me to hinder God's plans for my life, home, business, job, and education be nullified, exposed and destroyed in Jesus mighty name.

2) Every hired evil priest working day and night against my advancements in life, job, business, church, and ministry lose your job over my life and fail woefully in Jesus mighty name.

3) Every hidden satanic agent scattering all my efforts in life be exposed and destroy yourself in Jesus mighty name.

4) All satanic agents presenting evil evidences in satanic law-court against any area of my life by the authority in the blood of Jesus Christ lose your case or evidences against me and be scattered in Jesus mighty name.

5) Every arrow of evil tares secretly fired into any area of my life be exposed and burnt to ashes in Jesus mighty name.

6) Every hidden evil tree planted secretly into any area of my life through dreams be exposed and consumed by fire in Jesus mighty name.

7) By the authority in the blood of Jesus Christ, every satanic waster secretly assigned from evil case file to waste my productive years in life be exposed and wasted in Jesus mighty name.

8) Every destroyer assigned from evil case file secretly following me from childhood till now be exposed and destroyed from your secret place in Jesus mighty name.

9) Whatsoever is terminating any good thing coming into my life be terminated in Jesus mighty name.

10) Every satanic spy assigned against me from infancy to monitor and hinder my advancement, progress, or success be paralyzed and destroyed in Jesus mighty name.

11) Every satanic link with generational barrier from evil case file break off and be destroyed in Jesus mighty name.

12) Any secret sin in my life unknown to me withholding manifestation of God's plans for my life, be exposed and lose your ground against my life in Jesus mighty name.

13) Any hidden powers fertilizing and developing problems against any area of God's plans for my life, be exposed and be terminated in Jesus mighty name.

14) Any bridge that connects me with failures from my ancestors, collapse by through divine shakings and break into pieces in Jesus mighty name.

15) Every invisible hand from satanic kingdoms dropping seasonal problems into my life, be paralyzed and destroyed in Jesus mighty name.

16) All agents of darkness stationed at the doors of my advancement in life, ministry, church, business, and breakthroughs to resist God's plans for my life be paralyzed and destroyed in Jesus mighty name.

17) Any power that have collected the keys of my progress, success, church, and ministry through my dreams be paralyzed and release my keys in Jesus mighty name.

18) Every satanic and occult voice speaking barriers against my financial life, ministry, church and business be silenced and destroyed in Jesus mighty name.

19) Every diabolical man or woman on duty responsible for failure at the edge of success in any area of life, church, ministry, and breakthroughs be paralyzed and destroyed in Jesus mighty name.

20) Every satanic cobweb from evil network against God's plans upon my life, by the authority in the name of Jesus Christ, catch fire and be burnt to ashes in Jesus mighty name.

21) Every demonic agent planted within me, around me or my ministry, church, business, and job be exposed and scattered in Jesus mighty name.

CHAPTER SIX

Stronghold of Evil Prophecies

"For though we walk in the flesh, we do not war after the flesh:

*(For the weapons of our warfare are not carnal, **but mighty through God to the pulling down of strong holds;)***

Casting down imaginations, and every high thing that exalteth itself against the knowledge of God, and bringing into captivity every thought to the obedience of Christ;"

A. WHAT IS PROPHECY?

1) Prophecy is foretelling future events, or predicting what is to come. It is a declaration.

2) Prophecy is a divinely inspired prediction, instruction, or exhortation. A divinely inspired utterance

3) An inspired utterance or inspired declaration of divine will and purpose.

4) It is a statement that tells what will happen in the future

5) Godly *prophecy* is a message inspired by God, a divine revelation. The Bible says that *prophets "spoke as they were moved by Holy Ghost."* (2 Peter 1:20-21)

6) To prophesy is to predict something or to utter something inspired by God.

From this point forward we are looking at how to have total victory over every satanic stronghold against you through evil prophecies made against God's plans for your life. I am referring here to evil spoken word, negatives pronouncements, and wicked utterances inspired by satanic agents using some physical things which carry negatives forces to attack you.

Also those evil prophecies go with strongholds or poisons that can travel from one generation to another to accomplish the purpose in which it was released into the lives of some persons, families, and business, destinies, jobs, ministries, and churches. These negative or evil prophecies are released into people's lives through demonic agents into the air or through the media of dreams using human beings or animals which also has power to affect people's lives unknowingly.

To those people, the prophecy is channeled against them strengthened with strongholds of evil. The prophecy utterance released has controlling powers to manipulate people's daily lives, futures, business, and jobs. In addition, it goes with shadowing forces to influence people's daily lives thereby affecting every other thing that has to do with them. It is evil arrows with evil poisonous power injected into people's lives for evil missions in which if it is not spiritually discovered, rejected and destroyed, its manifestation would be fatal.

B. The Beginning of Godly Prophecy

In Genesis 1:3 the word of God ushers us into the beginning of God's prophetic utterance. *"And God said, Let there be light:* (Prophetic declaration) *and there was light."*

We see this prophetic declaration *"And God said,.."* in several verses of the scriptures. We see it repeated in verses 6, 9, 11, 14-15, 20, 24 and 26.

C. A Second Look At Prophecy

It is an inspired utterance or inspired declaration of divine will and purpose. For example in Isaiah 46:9-11 God's prophetic gift or the gift of prophecy is demonstrated.

"Remember the former things of old: for I am God, and there is none else; I am God, and there is none like me,

Declaring the end from the beginning, and from ancient times the things that are not yet done, saying, My counsel shall stand, and I will do all my pleasure:

Calling a ravenous bird from the east, the man that executeth my counsel from a far country: yea, I have spoken it, I will also bring it to pass; I have purposed it, I will also do it."

In Zech 10:1 we are advised to: *"Ask ye of the LORD rain in the time of the latter rain; so the LORD shall make bright clouds, and give them showers of rain, to every one grass in the field."*

This scripture is a declaration of God's promise, desire or will. Godly prophecy is a declaration of God's will upon our lives and environments too just like Jesus' model prayer, which includes the words *"...your kingdom come, your will be done on earth as it is in heaven"* (Matthew 6:10). This verse teaches that we should demand God's will in the world around us. As a modern-day prophets of God we speaks God's words "into the earth" or "into the atmosphere, "we believes that we can change our environment to conform to God's command and pave the way for God's purpose."

Prophetic prayer is believing that we are declaring the will God to happen; and we believe that it will actually create the thing declared by God's words from our mouth.

There are also satanic agents or satanic prophets speaking or declaring evil into people's lives, The bible warns against false prophets who claim to speak for God but who actually deceive the people they purport to inform.

King Ahab kept four hundred (400) such false prophets in his employment to tell him what he wanted to hear (2 Chronicles 18:4; 2 Timothy 4:3).

In the New Testament we have several warnings against false prophets. Jesus taught,

"Watch out for false prophets. They come to you in sheep's clothing, but inwardly they are ferocious wolves" (Matthew 7:15).

He later noted that, in the end times, *"false messiahs and false prophets will appear and perform great signs and wonders to deceive, if possible, even the elect"* (Matthew 24:24)

D. *MYSTERIOUS INSTRUMENTS OF PROPHECY*

In this section, we are going to look at some tools which ungodly prophets can use to make their evil declarations against peoples' lives. These are:

1) *THE SPEARS IN THE HANDS OF JOSHUA* - (**Josh. 8:18, 26**)

*"And the LORD said unto Joshua, **Stretch out the spear that is in thy hand toward Ai; for I will give it into thine hand**. And Joshua stretched out the spear that he had in his hand toward the city.*

Joshua drew not his hand back, wherewith he stretched out the spear, until he had utterly destroyed all the inhabitants of Ai."

The above scripture reveals to us that the power of God flowed into the spear in the hands of Joshua just like the rod in the hands of Moses.

Even these days we all know that Satan is a counterfeiter of whatsoever God does and he is still using those instruments through his agents all over the world in creating havocs in people's life.

2) *RODS OF MOSES AND AARON* - (Exodus 7:10-12)

"And Moses and Aaron went in unto Pharaoh, and they did so as the LORD had commanded: **and Aaron cast down his rod before Pharaoh, and before his servants, and it became a serpent.**

Then Pharaoh also called the wise men and the sorcerers: now the magicians of Egypt, they also did in like manner with their enchantments.

For they cast down every man his rod, and they became serpents: but Aaron's rod swallowed up their rods."

The rod is symbolic of support, strength rulership and dominion. God promised to send the rod of our strength from Zion in order for us to rule in the midst of our enemies (Ps 110:2). As you can see in the case of Aaron versus the magicians of Pharaoh, the rod of Aaron backed by God's power ruled in the midst of the enemies, by swallowing up all their rods.

The rod of God for dominion and rulership must be prayed for, so that God can release it to you in the place of prayer as we read in Psalm 110:2. Also in Psalm 2:8 for us to dominate the heathen with the rod of iron we must ask.

*"**Ask of me, and I shall give thee the heathen for thine inheritance, and the uttermost parts of the earth for thy possession. Thou shalt break them with a rod of iron; thou shalt dash them in pieces like a potter's vessel.**"*

You must ask so you can avoid the rod of the wicked from having authority over your life.

"For the rod of the wicked shall not rest upon the lot of the righteous; lest the righteous put forth their hands unto iniquity." (Psalm 125:3)

3) SATANIC ARROWS OF PROPHECY (Psalm 64:3)

Generally, arrows are weapons of war made out of wood and metal or wood shaft at the pointed end. They are also projectiles launched with bows. An arrow is useless without a bow to shoot.

Now, what arrow are we talking about here. Let's look at Psalm 64:3

"Who whet their tongue like a sword, and bend their bows to shoot their arrows, even bitter **words***:.."* (PS 64:3)

The arrows in focus here are bitter words and how are they released through the tongue. What do you use to shoot them? Your mouth. Evil prophets exercise the arrows of the tongue to afflict their innocent preys or victims!

4) SILENT EVIL PROPHECY: (Ezek 13: 1-3)

This is better explained through a profound verse of scriptures in Isaiah 8:19. These prophets are controlled by spirits that peep and mutter.

"And when they shall say unto you, Seek unto them that have familiar spirits, and unto wizards that peep, and that mutter: should not a people seek unto their God? for the living to the dead?"

They don't speak out loud and Ezekiel 13:2-3 further give us the picture of their operation:

"Son of man, prophesy against the prophets of Israel that prophesy, and say thou unto them that **prophesy out of their own hearts***, Hear ye the word of the LORD;*

Thus saith the Lord GOD; Woe unto the foolish prophets, that follow their own spirit, and have seen nothing!"

Furthermore, we see in Psalm 56:5 *"Every day they wrest my **words: all their thoughts are against me for evil."***

This simply means that these evil prophets can use the medium of negative meditation from their heart in firing poisonous arrows of destruction against people.

5) *FALSE DREAMS (Zech 10:2).*

They speak false dreams to deceive their vulnerable victims and operate in idolatry. They know what they see is a lie but they tell it all the same in order for the people to have their rest on a lie. While they give them false hope, the people are comforted in vain.

"For the idols have spoken vanity and the diviners have seen a lie, and have told false dreams; they comfort in vain: therefore, they went their way as a flock, they were troubled, because there was no shepherd."

But God has a strong word for them in Jeremiah 23:32:

"Behold, I am against them that prophesy false dreams, saith the LORD, and do tell them, and cause my people to err by their lies, and by their lightness; yet I sent them not, nor commanded them: therefore they shall not profit this people at all, saith the LORD."

6) *COMMERCIAL DIVINERS* (I Sam. 28:3, 7-8)

Saul the King sought one of these after the death of Samuel. He had no one to hear for him from God and he was desperate to seek for help from anyone who could so he went to the witch at Endor:

"Now Samuel was dead, and all Israel had lamented him, and buried him in Ramah, even in his own city. And Saul had put away those that had familiar spirits, and the wizards, out of the land.

Then said Saul unto his servants, Seek me a woman that hath a familiar spirit that I may go to her, and enquire of her. And his servants said to him, Behold, there is a woman that hath a familiar spirit at Endor.

And Saul disguised himself, and put on other raiment, and he went, and two men with him, and they came to the woman by night: and he said, I pray thee, divine unto me by the familiar spirit, and bring me him up, whom I shall name unto thee.

Also in Acts 16:16-18 we read about one of these people who followed Paul's team trying to gain attention by presenting the truth from the vessel of falsehood. This was sufficient to produce wrong perception about these men of God because the one introducing them was a veritable alien to truth. But thank God for the Spirit of the Lord who at the right season inspired Paul to cast out the evil spirit. Paul at this time was grieved and God intervened!

"And it came to pass, as we went to prayer, a certain damsel possessed with a spirit of divination met us, which brought her masters much gain by soothsaying:

The same followed Paul and us, and cried, saying, These men are the servants of the most high God, which shew unto us the way of salvation.

And this did she many days. But Paul, being grieved, turned and said to the spirit, I command thee in the name of Jesus Christ to come out of her. And he came out the same hour."

E. How to Be Victorious Over Strongholds of Evil Prophecies

1) You must repent from every known and unknown sin in your life and on behalf of your family because sin always lay the foundation for evil prophecies to take roots in people's life.

"Therefore thus saith the Lord GOD; Because ye have made your iniquity to be remembered, in that your transgressions are discovered,

51

so that in all your doings your sins do appear; because, I say, that ye are come to remembrance, ye shall be taken with the hand." (Ezekiel 21:24)

2) You must live the lifestyle of a prayer warrior by constantly praying and fasting.

3) Ask the Holy Spirit of God to reveal all areas of your life where strongholds of evil prophecies are working against you and nullify them.

"But the Comforter, which is the Holy Ghost, whom the Father will send in my name, he shall teach you all things, and bring all things to your remembrance, whatsoever I have said unto you." (John 14:26)

"Likewise the Spirit also helpeth our infirmities: for we know not what we should pray for as we ought: but the Spirit itself maketh intercession for us with groanings which cannot be uttered." (Romans 8:26)

4) You must reverse every known and unknown evil prophecy targeted at you at all times.

Prayers Against Evil Prophecies

1) Every stronghold of evil prophecy I have accidentally contacted from infancy and it's working against my life, be canceled and let your effects be destroyed in Jesus name.

2) Every history of evil prophecy running through my lineage working against my life be nullified and destroyed in Jesus mighty name.

3) Every destructive satanic prophecy advancing their wicked missions against any areas of my life be canceled and destroyed in the mighty name of Jesus.

4) Every daily destructive prophecy destroying every effort for my advancement in life be nullified and scattered in Jesus mighty name.

5) Every evil prophecy representing Goliath that is daily challenging God's plans for my life be silent forever and be scattered out of my life in Jesus mighty name.

6) Every defeat I'm going through as a reason of evil prophecy working against any area of my life be nullified and scattered in Jesus mighty name.

7) Any power supporting the operations of evil prophecy against God's plans upon my life collapse and be scattered in Jesus mighty name.

8) Every sacrifice empowering evil prophecies against any area of my life be destroyed in Jesus mighty name.

9) Every strongman or woman in charge of evil prophecy and all their small supporters be scattered and destroyed in Jesus mighty name.

10) All verbal prophecies, mental prophecies, silent prophecies and loud prophecies networking together against any area of my life be paralyzed and destroyed in Jesus mighty name.

11) Any destructive prophecy working in the place where I live be exposed and lose your power over my life in Jesus mighty name.

12) Whatsoever constitutes the operations of evil prophecy against any area of my life lose your ground and be destroyed in Jesus mighty name.

13) Any evil medical prophecy by any doctor against my health setting me up for early grave be nullified and canceled in Jesus mighty name.

14) Any wicked man or woman making incantations in any part of the world against my life, business, jobs, future, home, and family be scattered and destroyed in Jesus mighty name.

15) All wicked consultations with satanic prophets to gather evil evidences against me in order to open my life up to afflictions be nullified and scattered in Jesus mighty name.

16) Every seif-imposed prophecy I made in the past that has brought curses into my life be nullified and destroyed in Jesus mighty name.

17) Every satanic letter in circulation proclaiming judgment against me catch fire now in Jesus mighty name.

18) Every destructive prophecy made against my life through laying on of hands be nullified and destroyed in Jesus mighty name.

19) Every evil prophecy targeted at me from my infancy be nullified and destroyed in Jesus mighty name.

20) Every effect or consequence of destructive prophecies networking against any area of my life be nullified and scattered in Jesus mighty name.

21) Every power and evil personalities around me working to frustrate my advancements in life be exposed and destroyed in Jesus mighty name.

22) Any satanic prophecy that has established unending battles of life in any area of my ministry, church, business, jobs, and family be scattered and destroyed in Jesus mighty name.

23) By the authority in the blood of Jesus Christ, all playful evil pronouncement that my parents, friends, and relatives are issuing out of their mouth against me that are destructive prophecies be nullified and destroyed in Jesus mighty name.

24) I reject and reverse all evil destructive prophecies that I have consciously or unconsciously surrendered my life to in Jesus mighty name,

25) Any evil prophecy waiting for a particular time to attack my life, church, ministry, business, jobs, and future be exposed and scattered in Jesus mighty name.

26) By the authority in the blood of Jesus Christ, every evil prophecy issued against my life, career, jobs, future, ministry, church, and family by any agent of darkness be canceled and destroyed in Jesus mighty name.

27) By the authority in the blood of Jesus Christ, every witchcraft powers assigned to monitor any area of my life, career, job, and future scatter and be destroyed in Jesus mighty name.

28) All mysterious activities happening around me as a result of evil prophecy made against any areas of my life be nullified and paralyzed in Jesus mighty name.

29) Every stumbling block set against my advancements through evil prophetic pronouncements be nullified in Jesus mighty name.

30) Every mysterious object that has been used with evil prophecies against God's plans upon my life be nullified and scattered in Jesus mighty name.

31) Every mysterious cobweb working against my life, future, career, and family be scattered and destroyed in Jesus mighty name.

32) Any altar where destructive prophecy has been pronounced over my life be broken to pieces and scatter in Jesus mighty name.

33) Every altar of darkness erected to release evil prophecies over my life, and family be smashed to pieces in Jesus mighty name.

34) Any arrow of destruction fired at my life and family be scattered and destroyed in Jesus mighty name.

35) By the authority that is in the name of Jesus any evil rod or rods of satanic prophecy being used against any area of my life be broken to pieces and scattered in Jesus mighty name.

36) Every satanic hideout in and around my home, office, ministry, church, and business areas be exposed, nullified and scattered in Jesus mighty name.

37) Any wicked satanic priest commiss-ioned to pronounce evil prophecies over any area of my life, career, jobs, education, ministry, and church lose your power and be destroyed in Jesus mighty name.

38) Those I have given gifts and they are using them to make evil proclamations against my life, ministry, receive the judgments of God and be destroyed in Jesus mighty name.

39) Every satanic reinforcement deployed against any area of my life, and family to steal, kill, and destroy be paralyzed and destroyed in Jesus mighty name.

40) Any power reinforcing evil agenda against any areas of my life, and family be nullified and destroyed in Jesus mighty name.

41) Every sorcerer and occult agent upholding instruments of evil prophecies against my life be scattered and destroyed in Jesus mighty name.

42) By the authority in the name of Jesus every satanic mask built around my home, office business, ministry, and church be forcefully removed and destroyed in Jesus mighty name.

43) All strange satanic voices prophesying my downfall night and day be silenced and paralyzed now in Jesus mighty name.

44) Every flood of satanic attack released from evil altars against any area of my life, future, career, jobs, by the authority in the blood of Jesus Christ be paralyzed in Jesus mighty name.

45) All satanic armed robber delegated to come and steal, kill and destroy all my efforts in life be paralyzed in Jesus mighty name.

46) In the name of Jesus all satanic prophecies forcing my life backwards by the authority in the blood of Jesus Christ I frustrate your operations over my life now.

47) All evil prophecies and predictions made against me from my childhood be nullified and destroy in Jesus mighty name.

48) In the name of Jesus every hidden covenant and vow of affliction made by my father and mother but now working against my life and family I command you to be nullified and paralyzed in Jesus mighty name.

49) By the authority that is in the blood of Jesus Christ, every satanic embargo and sanctions from wicked altars networking against any areas of my life, future, career, jobs, ministry, and church be paralyzed and destroyed in Jesus mighty name.

50) Every door of opportunities presently shut by evil prophecies spoken from any evil altar against my life, future, business, career, ministry, church, and education be opened now in Jesus mighty name.

ABOUT THE AUTHOR

Reverend, Dickson I. Samuel is the founder and president of Living Victorious Life International Ministry Inc. with the headquarters in Dallas, Texas U.S.A. and branches in Nigeria.

Rev. Dickson Ifeanyi Samuel is a faith based teacher and preacher of the unadulterated word of God. He started his heavenly journey back in Africa under Rev. O. Ezekiel of Christian Pentecostal Mission (C.P.M), at a crusade in Aba in 1989 and from then on the fire of the Holy Ghost that fell on him during that crusade never dissipated. He has never turned back since then and by the special grace of God he will continue till eternity.

He began his ministry work serving at the CPM Headquarter, Ajao Estate, Lagos in 1990, and where he also bagged Bachelor's Degree in Theology with Pentecostal International Bible Seminary (PIBS). He thereafter, attended Lagos State University (LASU) with Diploma in Theology

After his studies, he was sent to be the pastor of some of the branches of CPM, before the Lord sent him on another level of his divine mandate to establish the Redeemed Solid Faith Mission in October, 2001

Rev. Dickson Ifeanyi Samuel began his global ministry after visiting the Holy Land, Israel in 2003, and since then he has been on a global stage ministering in conferences, churches and seminaries all over the world. He is a man of prayers and gifted in the areas of healing and deliverance with signs and wonders following.

Rev, Dickson Ifeanyi Samuel is a pastor of pastors, a man with great passion to see other ministers blessed and succeed as well. He is the current International President of Igbere Ministers Global Forum (I.M.G.F) and also Global Ministers Network Fellowship (G.M.N.F). He is also a community development minded man of God, and the facilitator of the ongoing Igbere Secondary School Renovation Projects.

Through God's leading he established Igbere Ministers Global Forum, a Platform that has gathered all Igbere indigenous ministers from churches and denominations within Igbere community for the purpose of bringing spiritual succor and development to Igbere Community. He gives scholarship to some Igbere children. He is married and blessed with children.

Printed in the United States
By Bookmasters